HOWLERS

HOWLERS

William Cooke
with illustrations by Mike Gordon

FREDERICK MULLER
London Sydney Auckland Johannesburg

First published in Great Britain in 1988 by Frederick Muller
an imprint of Century Hutchinson Ltd, Brookmount House,
62-65 Chandos Place, London WC2N 4NW

Century Hutchinson, Australia Pty Ltd
89-91 Albion Street, Surry Hills, NSW 2010, USA

Century Hutchinson, New Zealand Ltd
PO Box 50-086, Glenfield, Auckland 10, New Zealand

Century Hutchinson, South Africa (Pty) Ltd
PO Box 337, Bergvlei 2012, South Africa

British Library Cataloguing in Publication Data

Howlers.
1. Children's humorous quotations in
English, 1945- – Anthologies
I. Cooke, William. II. Gordon, Mike
082

ISBN 0-09-17395-1

Printed and bound in Great Britain by
Anchor Brendon Ltd, Tiptree, Essex

Contents

Acknowledgments

For allowing me to use material quoted in their examiners' reports, I am indebted to the Joint Matriculation Board, the London Chamber of Commerce and Industry, the Royal Society of Arts Examinations Board, the West Midlands Examinations Board and the Associated Examining Board (* indicates quotations from the Chief Examiner's Report AEB).

I should also like to thank Marling School and the many colleagues and friends who have contributed to this book, especially Ian Butterworth, John Hawthorne and Alan Murray.

Extracts from Section 3 were first published in *The Guardian*.

Locusts is Incests
(Odd Jottings)

The three angels in the Creation were Raphael, Gabriel and Urinal.

Women are no longer having as many children due to a higher standard of loving.*

The angel Gabriel came down from Heaven and gave Mary a massage.

Before birth it is advisable to visit an anti-natal clinic.

It is alright for mothers to go out to work before they have children.

The average family size is 2.2. What is .2 of a child? – usually a dog.*

When we are born we are given a status, that is you are either a boy or a girl or something your parents have passed on.

The more intelligent the child the sooner it will reach sanitation and turn off the TV.*

Minor faults can be discovered and corrected in pregnancy, but a mongrel child cannot be corrected.*

The biblical cord is then cut by the midwife that has been responsible for everything passed between the mother and the foetus.

Young babies, left on doorsteps, take a big step backward in life.*

One mother who adopted a Vietnamese baby took language lessons so that she could understand the child when it grew up.

Immigrants often do not bother to learn to speak the English Language let alone wright it.

Grate Britt'n has the best educain cistern in the wold.*

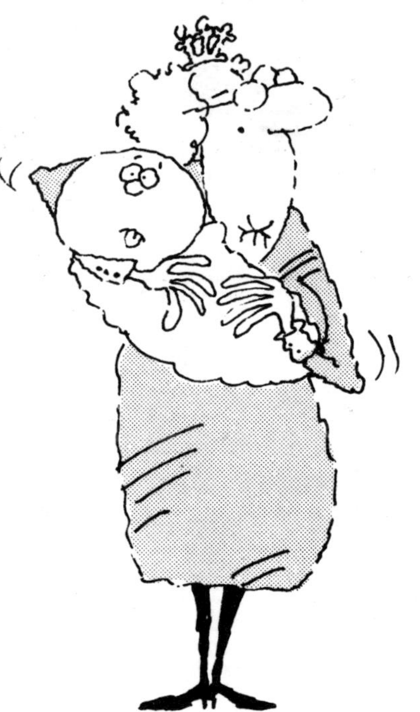

Rich families do better with their children because they can afford an old peer girl.*

Dear Sir,

Veronica was absent with permission because her sister had a baby. Please thank the Headmaster very much.

Dear Miss,

Bobby will not be comming to school today on account of a billiards attack.

[illegible]

Tomorrow it is spots day. The Lord Mare is coming to give out the prizes.

You must have an ordination before joining the school choir.

If there was no scool rools there would be utercayoss.

(Question in class) ‘How many ‘O’ levels do I need for soliciting?’

(Teacher to class)
'Now watch the board while I go through it.'

This is a specticcill not to be mist.

School daze are the happiest daze of your life.

Capital punishment would teach them a lesson they'd remember for the rest of their lives.

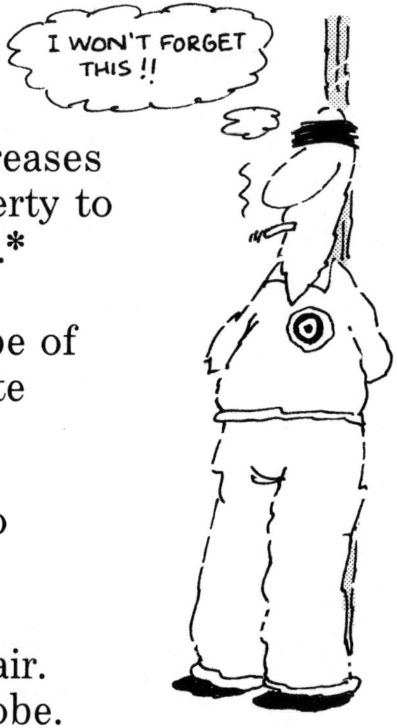

Q. State one change in boys at puberty.
A. His vice deepens.

The brain increases in size at puberty to hold emotions.*

To vote you must be over the age of eighteen and be of fixed mind, meaning that you are not stupid and vote Conservative because it has a nice ring to it.

The cost of living is rising with youngsters having to spend more money on essentials like pop records.*

Q. Briefly describe how to carry out any simple repair.
A. To mend a puncha stick a plasta on the in a choobe.

For the party the girl wore a mini skirt and a lovely manure blouse.

There was rough crockery on the shelves and rough mating on the floor.

Adultery is more likely if you're not married.*

While wiping her eyes, the organ burst forth into the strains of the Wedding March.*

The story in the Book of Ruth was written to oppose the terrible jokes concerning mothers-in-law that the Lord foresaw.*

There is one major sports centre – everything can be done here: judo, karate and all the other marital arts.

Marriage is the main cause of divorce.

A Christian couple can get divorced, but not Roman Catholics.*

Q. Give one word for 'a man with two wives'.
A. Pigamist.

The Old Testament was written 1,000 years ago and the New Testament 100 years ago.*

The rubble is the currency in Russia.

Jews go and pray at the Whaling Wall.*

The perpetual light over the ark in the synagogue is kept there in case of power cuts.

The West Midlands includes Dudley and the rest of the Dark Country.

The communists are called the Walsall packed countries.

Q. Name the German national airline.
A. The Luftwaffe.

Wie arrive hast dem Airport vor dem Aeroplane. Der Luggage ist checked hast dem Customs. Wie board der Plane about 12 noon . . .

Juan Carlos is Spain's most famous bullfighter.

One of the natural resources of Switzerland is the cuckoo clock.

Inter alia – an Italian airline operating in most parts of the world.

Q. Name one of Italy's historic monuments.
A. The Leaning Tower of Pizza.*

Food handlers should keep their fingers cut short.

An Arab is a man with a turbine on his head.

Man is only a nackered ape.

Amphibians can walk on both land and water.*

Q. What is an animal with a backbone called?
A. A vibrator.

DOES THIS MEAN WE'RE ENGAGED?

Dogs usually propose by urinating.*

Bacteria are important because if there were no bacteria then there would be no diseases of any kind, so bacteria are needed.

Sleeping sickness is brought on by the bite of the sexy fly.

The diver knew he had to act quickly when the octopus wrapped its testacles around him.

Fortune-tellers believe they are sidekick.*

Some people have extra-sensual perception.*

Mrs Whitehouse runs a highly effective incest group.*

Weightlessness can be produced by over-dieting.*

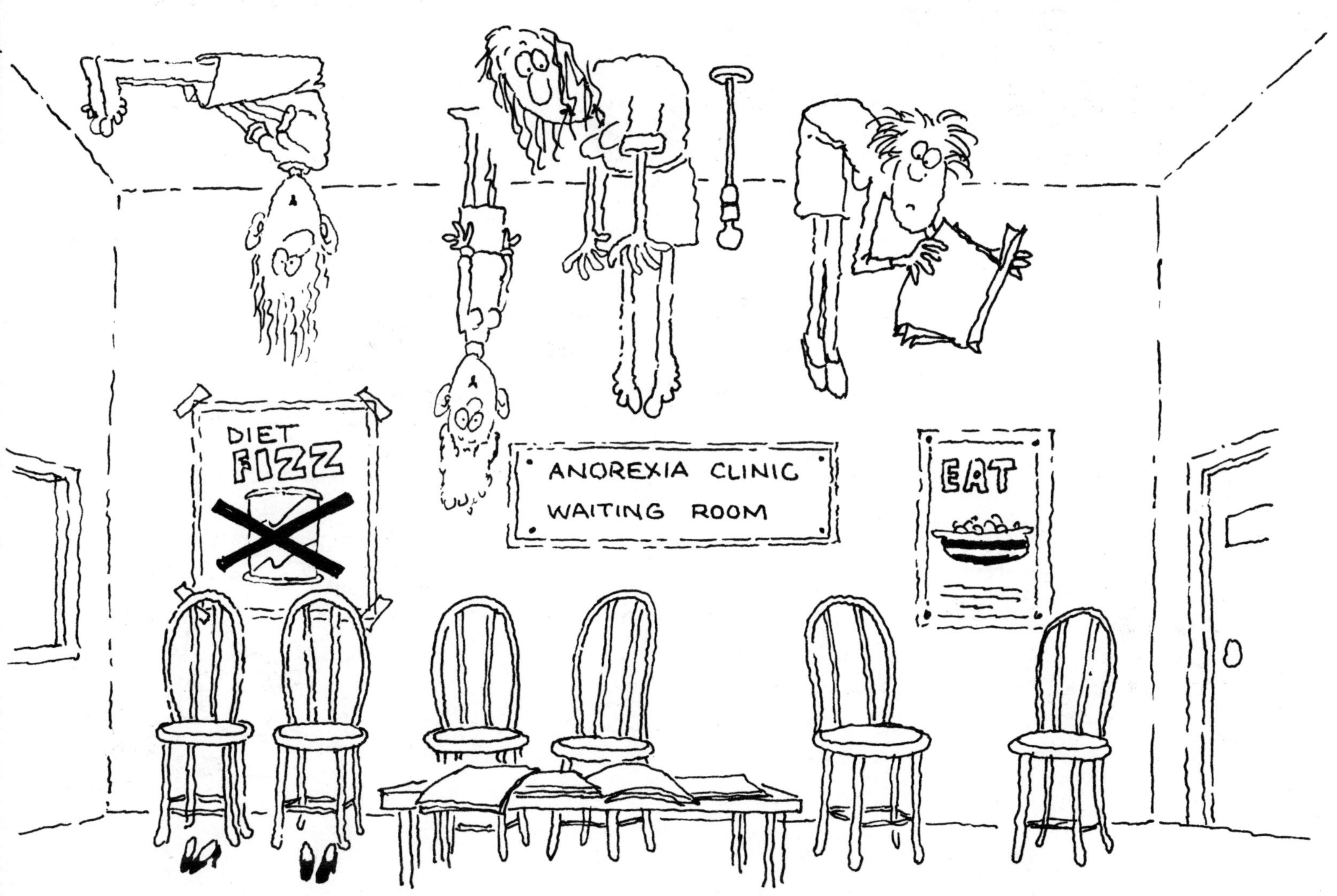

Pollution is caused by cars giving off intoxicating fumes.

The war victim returned armed with an artificial leg.*

It has been said that both NHS and private patients will soon be sharing the same bed.

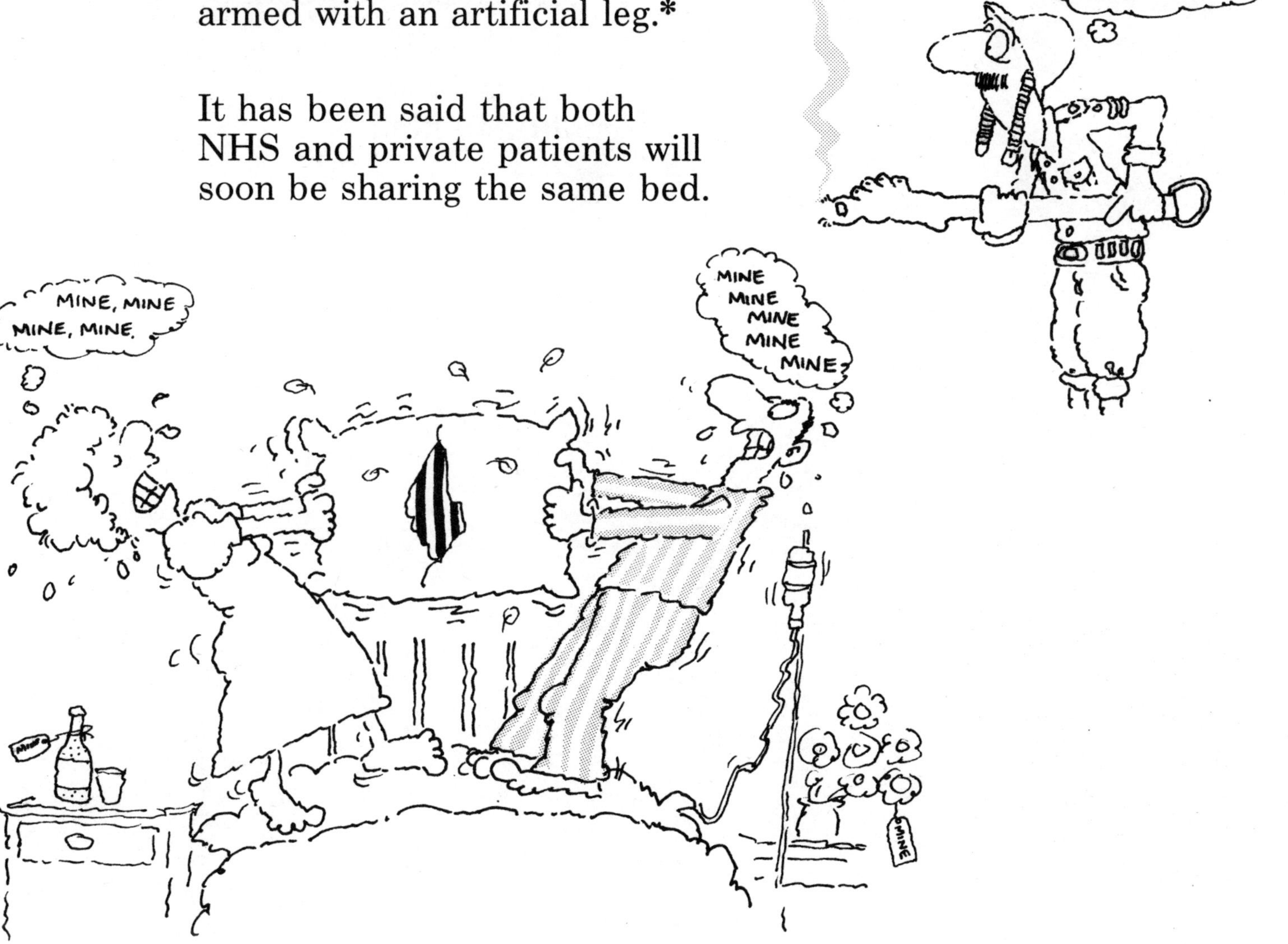

An atheist is someone who puts you to sleep before an operation.

Euthanasia, in the wrong hands, could be lethal.*

A cardiograph tells you when you are dead.*

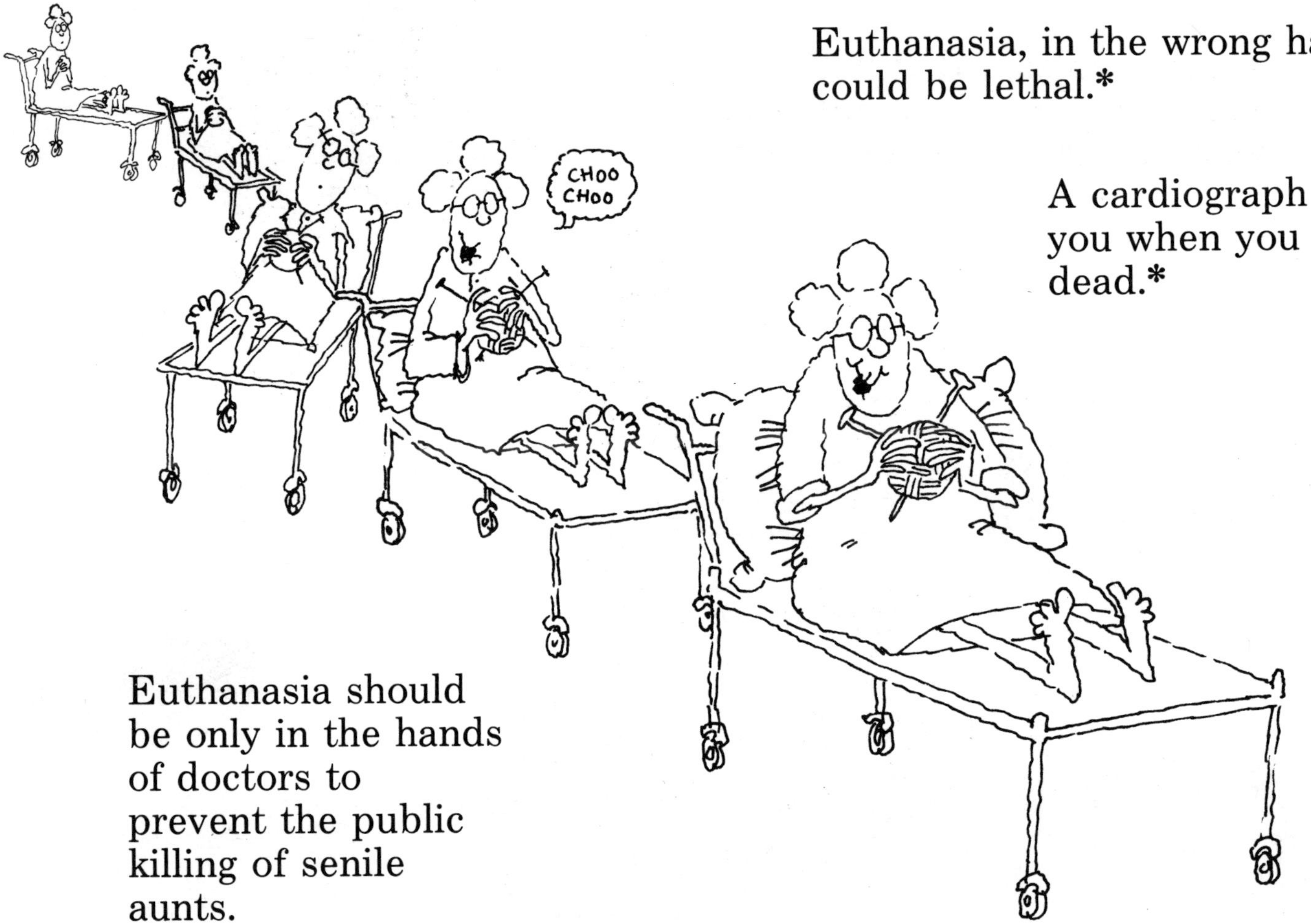

Euthanasia should be only in the hands of doctors to prevent the public killing of senile aunts.

The deceased was very quiet in the court room.

Stipendiary Magistrates are more severe as they have to justify their salary.

Reasonable chastity is permitted by the law.

Balstalls are places to which young men are sent if they have done something that is not too bad.*

People can be sued for liable and deformation of character.

If you start from the same point on the earth's axis and go round both ways at the same time, you will eventually meet yourself.

The Chairman announced that the record player was not available because it had been smashed by parsons unknown.

Pheasants on bicycles . . .

(History Ancient and Modern)

In Ancient Egypt when a woman died she was stuffed with herbs to restore her, then she was raped in a sheet and became a mummy.

The Anglo-Saxons weren't as dumb as many people think although most could not read or write, but who needed to when you were raping and pillaging?

Alfred was scolded for burning some cakes but he kept his cool.

The Venereal Bede did much to improve our knowledge.

Vikings were good sea-fairies.

In 1066 Harold, hearing of the Danish invasion, collected his army and marched up the route of the A1.

(Battle of Stamford Bridge) Tostig and Hardrada were both killed in a battle which was called the Battle of Chelsea.

The Battle of Haystrings was fought in 1066.

The Norman soldiers were very enthusiastic during William's coronation since they burned some nearby houses to light up the scene.

William Rufus was hit by an arrow and circumcised.

(Medieval justice) You threw a man tied hands and feet into a pond; if he sank he was innocent, but if he sunk he was guilty.

Tenants-in-chief had to swear filthy to the King.

Conway Castle is a good example of medieval agriculture.

A medieval villein in the true sense was not free for he was tied to the ground.

Archbishop Anselm fled to France, not returning into History until Henry I's reign.

The ordeals of a knight involved rescuing damsels in distress.

(The Constitutions of Clarendon) Henry II said that a priest who committed a crime must be judged in the church court and undressed.

Thomas Becket died a mater.

(The Crusading Period) Crucifixes were put up along all the main highways of Europe. Someone with a religious burden could merely kneel down to relieve himself.

The King met the Barons at Runnymede for the Great Chatter.

John was a stubborn and a headless king.

After Becket was killed, a woman who was ill dipped her handkerchief into his blood and was cured. After this Lourdes became a place of pilgrimage.*

Edward II was not fit to be a king. Whenever a tournament was going on, he and Piers Gaveston would play dice and other games in the stables.

The Black Death was brought by ships from the Black Sea.

. . . NO YOU IDIOT, I SAID BRING BACK BETH! . . .

(Another) The Black Death was a warning from God and this brought on masochistic activities such as a great wave of flatulence.

After the Black Death there was another plague known as the Black Prince.

(One effect of the Black Death) Cows were mooing their heads off for want of being milked.

(Deposition of Richard II) When Richard returned to England his men were dispersed, and as he reached Flint Castle he saw Henry Bolingbroke with a magnanimous force.

The Black Prince died of an immortal disease.

The Lollards did not do much; they chanted hymns and lolled around.

Henry IV married with a French lady. It was indeed comic to hear the conversation of husband and wife, one speaking English and the other French. Their products were bastards, as we should say.

Henry was a very shrewd man and did not punish the imposter Simnel but made him a turnip in the palace kitchen.

The Diet of Worms took place in the reign of Martin Luther King.

Joan of Arc was burnt to a steak.

Henry VII saved the kingdom from an archy.

Henry V claimed the French throne by declaring himself the great grandson of his father.

Henry VII was the first European king to maintain the power of balance.

Columbus knelt down, thanked God, and put the American flag in the ground.

In the reign of Henry VI we come across a certain man called Warwick the Kingmaker. He was very powerful and very useful to anyone who wanted to become king.

Henry wanted his marriage to Catherine of Aragon to be declared dull and void.

Cardinal Wolsey was sent to the block, but God was in his favour so that he was wearied during his travels and died at Leicester, thus escaping the Blockhead's men.

The dissolution of the monasteries left the country full of vagrant bishops.*

(Tudor social problems) There was a great increase in crime as many bishops could not find work.

Elizabeth made Walter Raleigh one of her nights.

The Massacre of Bartholomew was a brutal attack on innocent publicans.*

This unknown air Elizabeth possessed earned her the nickname of 'Black Bess' or 'Dark Horse'.

Drake said that the Armada could wait but his bowels couldn't.

After the death of Elizabeth, she named James as her heir.

James was a man with a stabowy mouth and a wrigity walk.

Charles was executed for the first time in 1649.*

(War of the Spanish Succession) The English wanted to put the Arch-Duck on the Spanish throne.

George II was an extremely fussy little man, bursting with marital ardour.

John Wesley was the son of a Methodist minister. He traversed the countryside on his bicycle.

Peter the Great westernised Russia by building cinemas and music halls.*

John Kay was the first man to make a Flying Scuttle.

The Agrarian and Industrial Revolutions had left the minds of the peasants in a turmoil. They did not know whether they were standing on their heads or their heels, and until this had been sorted out there would be great discomfort among them.

Q. Name any leader of the French Revolution.
A. Rubberspear.

The cause of the French Revolution was that the peasants had to pay three taxis.

Napoleon's first assignment was at the storming of the Bastille. He was told to stop the mob charging. He placed his artillery in the street and as the mob charged, he ordered his guns to be fired. Although the grapefruit killed quite a number of people, it stopped the charging mob. He was praised for this tough assignment.

King Louis didn't bother that the peasants were starving – he just stayed in the palace and kept on holding his balls.

(1812) Napoleon said ‘This isn’t our best season – we’ll try again next year.’

After Waterloo Napoloen went to St Helens to dye.

One of the terms of the Congress of Vienna enabled all illegitimate kings to be restored to their thrones.

AND BEFORE YOU GO, GENTLEMEN, ________ !!

(The Quadruple Alliance, 1815) The Powers of the Alliance promised that they would not do anything without insulting each other.

The Dutch in the early 19th century faced financial crises because of the costly war between Holland and Netherland.

In the 19th century bronchitis was very popular.

An Education Act passed near the middle of this period increased the period of learning by lengthening the numbers of hours in the day.

Many improvements were made in France during the reign of Louis XVIII. In 1820 the Duc de Berry was murdered.

Women in the 19th century were regarded as men.

Florence Nightingale was famous for her work in the Korean War.

In Italy Gary Baldy and his Gorillas rode to victory.

Bismarck was a porn-broker at the Congress of Berlin.*

In his second ministry Gladstone, a well-known believer in lost causes, tried even harder to improve the conditions of the Irish.

Gladstone's association with Parnell and the disastrous result of their adultery helped discredit Gladstonian policies.*

What upset the Victorians most was the thought of their descendants being apes.

(Birth of the Co-op) The Rochdale Pioneers opened a wholesale grousers' shop.

After the 1905 Russian Revolution cheap trips were laid on for those who wanted to emigrate to Siberia.*

One of the most famous suffragettes was Lady Astor who threw herself off the Queen's horse at Hickstead.*

At the turn of the century the poorer people in towns had no amusements except dice or maybe marbles or a hoola hoop if one could be found.

America threatened to enter the First World War when a U-boat sank Lithuania.*

Mrs Pankhurst threw herself under the King's horse at the Grand National but it was only a publicity stunt for the television cameras.*

In 1917 a Labour politician was taken into Lloyd George's Wall Cabinet.

The great war ended in 1918. We have had two minutes of peace every year since then.

The Weimar constitution gave the vote to all consenting males.*

The Latrine Treaty was concluded in 1919 between Mussolini and the Pope.*

One of the conditions of the Lateran Treaty was that Mussolini would marry the daughter of the Pope.*

Q. Who said ‘I pledge myself to a new deal for the American people’?
A. Stalin.

In the 30s the unemployed went on hunger marches from Harrow.

(September 1938) Hitler took over the Sudetenland and all the Sudanese living there.

Hitler's stormtroopers were affectionately known as the SS.

The Allies perfected a bouncing bomb and used it against large German dames.*

The atomic bomb was first dropped on Bombay.

Birmingham was invaded by Russian tanks in 1953 at the request of its government.

The Vietnam war went on under David Nixon with pheasants on bicycles bringing supplies along the Ho Chi Min trail.*

Magellan circumcised the world with his 40 foot clipper.

From the wife of bath to 007

(A Potty Guide to English Literature)

Chaucer invented the English Language.*

(*The Prologue*) The Prioress is 'amyable of port' – friendly after she'd had a drop.

The Monk is riding a fine horse which proves he has broken his vow of chastity.

The Wife of Bath never complained except when she was raped by three friars.

The Doctor of Physique is well heeled.

Miracle plays were performed in the navel.*

Mystery plays were made popular by Agatha Christie.

As a youth Shakespeare spent a year under Queen Elizabeth.

In *A Midsummer Night's Dream* Lysander and Demetrius have succumbed to Hernia.

The deaths in *Romeo and Juliet* were very life-like.

Q. Who was Juliet's father?
A. Lord Catapult

Q. Who was Juliet's mother?
A. Lady Copulate

When planning Caesar's assassination Brutus said it should be done with dignity, not in a sworded manner.

Mark Antony, the playboy, has an excellent grasp of pubic affairs.

In *Henry IV, Part 2* Shakespeare alternates comic and serious scenes. This is to bring the audience out of a deep state of depression and prepare them for more depression.*

Marcellus was write when he wrote that something was wrotten in the state of Denmark.

. . . or ere this
I should have fatted all the region kites
With this slave's offal.

Hamlet feels he should have already achieved revenge and used the king's skin to make kites for everyone in the state.

It is mainly Hamlet's actions that lead people to believe him mad – appearing and frightening Ophelia in her bedroom with his trousers round his ankles.

Hamlet stabs through the arras. It was curtains for Polonius.

When we first meet the MacBeths, they are quite an ordinary couple.

The verse of *King Lear* is in prose.

Lear suffered a great deal from Reagan . . .
and Gonorrhoea.

He was advised to take pomp and physics. ('Take physic, Pomp . . .')

Antony and Cleopatra is full of phallic cymbals.

Cleopatra killed herself by taking aspic . . .
and died in her needle.

I found the play difficult to understand due to it being written in Shakespeare.

(*The White Devil*) Flamineo is a panda.*

Masques were designed by Indigo Jones.*

(*Samson Agonistes*) Samson knows the Bible so well he can quote it.

The Restoration Theatre was so called because its roof was being restored.*

As he grew older Wordsworth went out one evening because he felt the call of nature.

Wordsworth was obsessed with Nature. One night he went to Lake Windermere and just sucked it all up.

The alliteration of ‘wild west wind’ gives Shelley’s poem a breezy opening.

Keats uses words to enhance his style.

Jane Eyre falls in love with Rochdale.

Jane Austen reaches her climax through a series of deft touches.

Byron's prose is painstakingly written as if in a hurry.*

(*Great Expectations*) Mrs Joe is killed by being hit on the head with a convict's leg.

Tom Sawyer was written by Mark Twain whose real name was Samuel Pepys.

(*The Mayor of Casterbridge*) Lucetta is a croquette.*

(*Tess of the D'Urbervilles*) After committing Alec's murder, Angel accompanies Tess to Starveacre and on their way they are involved in a pagan sacrificial ritual with a stone.

Pygmalion is a story about a curnel Pickerin, proficient Higgin and a flour girl.

(*Sons and Lovers*) Paul realises that Miriam loves him because of her French letter.

James Bond is the most famous secret agent ever erected.

(*A Handful of Dust*) With Tony in the jungle, Brenda is having a wail of a time; Rosa looks like Brenda, according to Tony, who is wearing a floral dress.

A Select Reading List

Hammer's *Oddity*

Gray's *Allergy*

'The Pied Piper of Hamlet'*

David Bellamy's *Origin of Species*

Owen's 'Dulc de Crum Es Pro Patrick Moore'

Orwell's *Dining Out in Paris and London*

Larkin's 'Anthem for Doomed Youth on Beaulieu Water'

TO BEE
OR NOT TO
BEE

Ride of the Vultures

(Music)

Mozart was born at the age of five.

The first performance of Handel's *Messiah* was given a standing ovation.

Mozart's father was called Leopard Mozart.

Mozart and Haydn wrote for performances in saloons.*

The great Romantic, J.S. Bach, gave way to the Baroque Beethoven as the leading English composer of the eighteenth century.*

Beethoven had little education so he made up his money by teaching.

Beethoven wrote nine symphonies and he only heard of them as he became deaf.

Berlioz had a spilt personality.

Berlioz loved tubular belles.

Debussy's first works were often half romantic and half impressionist because his emotion got the better of him . . . He suspended a note in mid-air and left it there, and this created his symbolist art.

Tchaikovsky was taught at the Conservatoire by Frankenstein.

Elvis Presley was a more refined pop star than Bill Haley. Many of the rock stars were idles to the youngsters. Today there are different categories of pop – from 'Sole' to 'Punk'.

(Elgar's *Enigma Variations*)
The first limb appears with the bassoon in small sections.

It is followed by an arabesque backwards.

Famous Works

The Coronation Anthem
Zorba the Greek

Bach's *Staccato and Fugue in D minor*

Mendeloon's *The Hebrides Overture*

Handel's *Lager*

Wogart's *Ride of the Vivaldis*

Wogan's *Fly of the Voldukeries*

The Dance of the Sugar Prune Fairy

Bikini's *Madame Butterfly*

Some Terms Defined

pesante – like a peasant

col legno – with the leg

𝅗𝅥. spotted minim

♩. dotted croquet

♩ = 76 means 76 seconds to the crotchet

♮ is not a sharp, nor a blunt, but in between

A rondo is a light and heated form.

Major keys sound smooth; minor keys sound bumpy.

Modes are middle-aged songs.

A grace note gets in the way.

Double stopping – that is while one little tune is being played in the background another tune much more elaborate in style is being played, both on the same violin.

The baboon is the lowest woodwind instrument.

The piano trio consists of a piano, drums and a Dublin bass.

A Requiem Mass is the end of the world.

The trumpist is in the brass section.

Crushendo – an orchestra for everyone to join in.

Gated by a pretentious toilet

(French life, language, letters)

The French National Anthem is called ‘The Mayonnaise’.

"La crême de la saladecrême"

Q. Name any French politician.
A. Charles de Ghoul.

Les Français boirent café au lay . . .
et mangent les caisses de grenouilles.

Snails are classified into scrag, rump and middle neck.

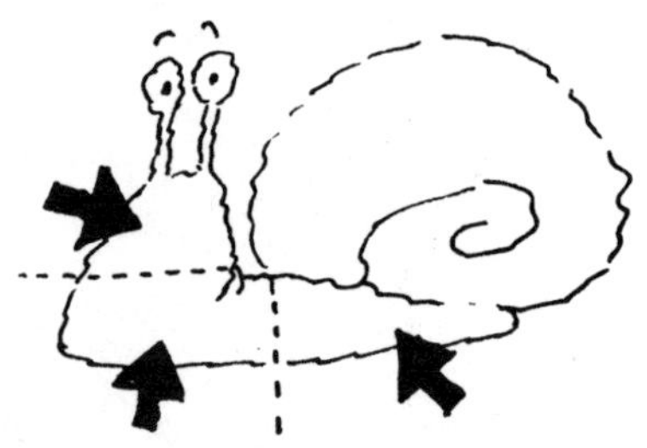

Q. Name a French cheese.
A. Danish blue
   Caerphilly
   Canonball

Pension complète – old-age pensioners pay full rate.

The Louvre is a well-known night-club.

When you get on a French bus the conductor will punch a hole in it.

The bus was travelling at 400 km an hour, more than the road signs allowed.

The Mont St Michel is a large mound which travels out to sea.

The River Seine has a left bank on one side.

Il a vu des actrices charmantes mais gâtées par une toilette prétentieuse.
– He saw some charming actresses gated by a pretentious toilet.

Q. Name a French winter sport.
A. Bog-slaying.

Je suis fiancé. C'est la guerre.
– I am engaged to a gorilla.

Des nuées[1] traversaient l'horizon.
– Naked women are crossing the horizon.

Saucisses – saucy girls.

Un roman policier[2] qui la passionnait . . .
– A Roman policeman took her passionately . . .

A French policeman has a little office in the middle of the street.

Q. Name any French tourist attraction.
A. The Highfull Tower
Arc de Trump
Madame Twoswords

[1] clouds
[2] a detective novel

A spaniard in the works...

(The Business World)

Personnel

The prophet of a company is very important.

If a partner cannot pay his debts, a court will order a bayleaf to eject him from his house.

Perks are things that make directors happy like pretty girls.

A stag is a man who works in the Stock Exchange chasing other men.

One type of accountant in a firm is the Turf Accountant.

A work study engineer shows how reproduction can be more efficient.

The Office Supervisor felt that the secretaries, with their morals boosted, would achieve a greater output of work.

The store-keeper should have a good pilfering system.

The Trade Unions have joint consultation with management for a couple of hours and then a full-scale row.

Another name for a shop steward is ‘mother superior’.

The Secretary Bird

A Company Secretary takes the minutes and makes the tea.

Audio-typists are supervised by a dictator.

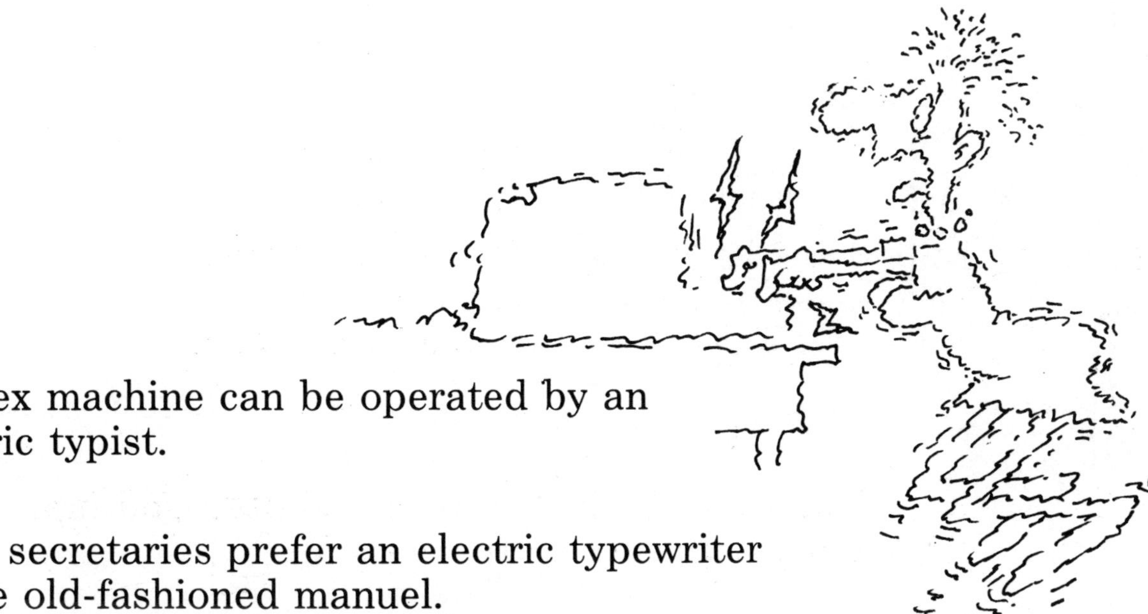

A telex machine can be operated by an electric typist.

Most secretaries prefer an electric typewriter to the old-fashioned manuel.

A secretary is often a Director's private concern.

Her duties can be very embracing for her boss.

Previous tempting work is an advantage.

She usually begins the day by sorting out the male.

Another of her duties is to file correspondents.

The word processor has a 'curser' for when the secretary makes a mistake.

The secretary just presses a button and in a minute appears on the screen.

A good telephone manor is essential. She should not just pick up the receiver and say 'Hell'.

At meetings the minuets are an important aspect of her work.

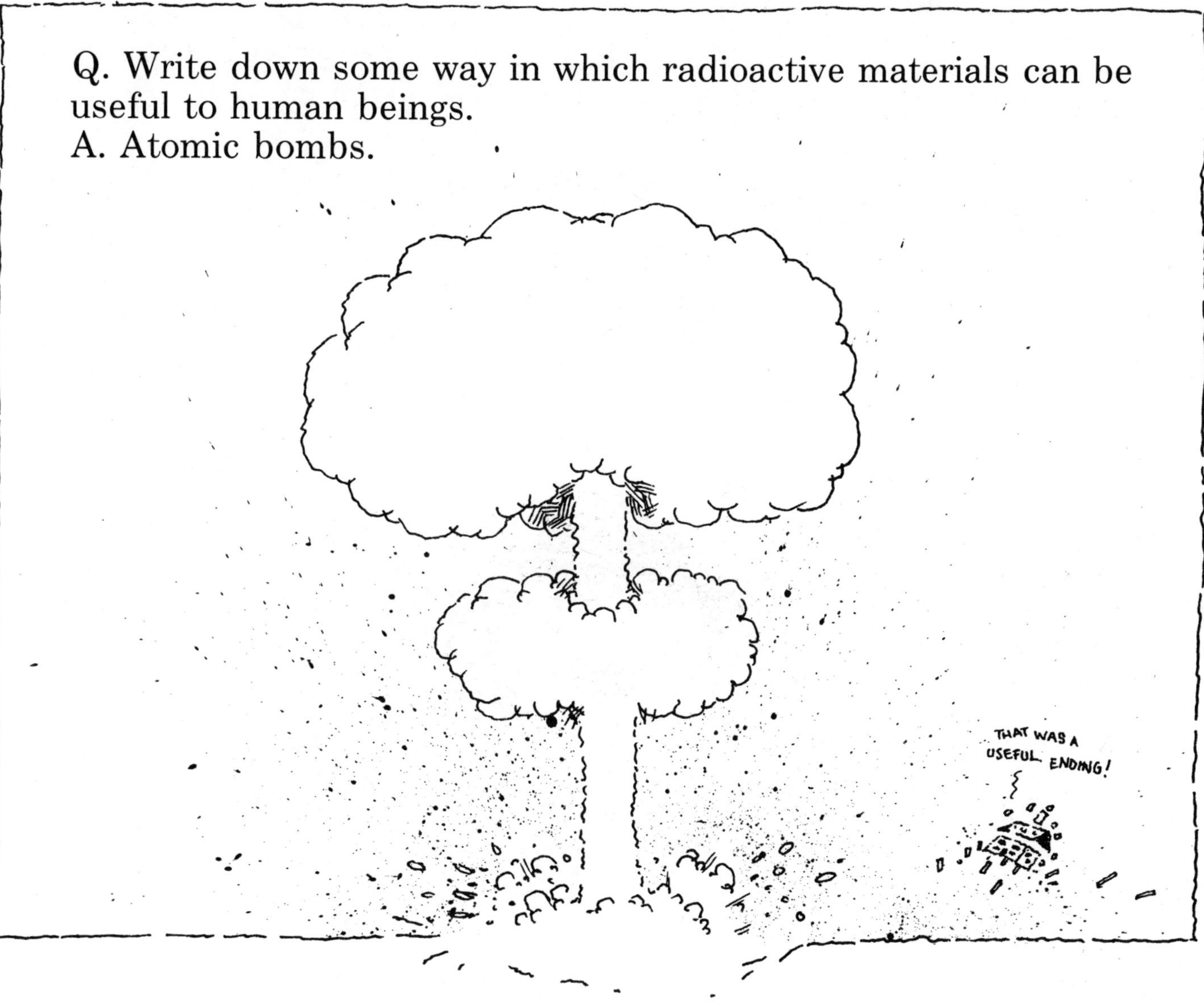
Q. Write down some way in which radioactive materials can be useful to human beings.
A. Atomic bombs.
THAT WAS A USEFUL ENDING!

EXAMS DO PUT
ENORMUS STAINS
ON YOU!